CITY
IN THE LAND OF
NOD

BY SAMULI LAMPINEN

© Samuli Lampinen 2013

Layout: Anssi Muurimäki

Translation terminator: Miisa Passila

Published by BoD – Books on demand GmbH,
Helsinki, Finland

Printed by BoD – Books on Demand GmbH,
Norderstedt, Germany

ISBN: 978-952-286-649-3

I

KOLMANSKOP

Diamonds are not eternal. Greed is a

permanent reminder of
how weak we were.

I am still digging my mind
to find a god
who would be a humanist.

And
there will be blood.

Hanoi

Only very few people ever want to
be the first ones in something
before afterwards.
Even less ever will. To be free

from the slavery
of other's freedom
is enough for a warrior,

but too much for the soldiers
who follow their flag
and win all the battles in its name
by sacrificing their freedom to it.

Moyale

The borderline between union and mayhem
can be thin and clear sometimes
like the bridge I crossed yesterday.

Fighting parties were withdrawn to the hills earlier
and now security forces control the town
with the sticks they use as they pleased
among civilians.

At today's rate
one mark of Abel
equals one hundred and eight
of Cain's.

BULAWAYO

An unarmed police points in two directions.
Either the country is safe as hell
or his excellency the President thinks it's no longer
a heaven for him.

Sun sets, sun rises.
Time sets

a constant euphemism for the shadows
on one's face.

Luxor

If you desire to be a prophet
in your own land,
carve a statue
and build a colorful home, paramount
to all the religious kitsch;
build a tomb

for the independence of thought.

Bones of the prophet
testify that promised land
will remain
intact, will remain
a mirage of permanence
in the sand.

Lüderiz

I am sitting in the shadow
of the lighthouse
looking at blind ships floating
in the windy bay.

I don't try to find a difference
between beach and desert anymore.
Thinking of something which doesn't exist
is a waste of time

in the abundance of space. Nothing less
and the whole beauty of it.

AGRA

Moment takes its time
in the shadows of the nine planets,
because it carts a sun
for all of them.

Four white pillars
in two rows,
three colors – black

gnawing this camera
to its very bone.

Sedgefield

In the core of pain
is loneliness,

little bit butter
in the wing of the fly.

HARARE

A dream breaths heavily
in the dim light of a hungry mosquito.

Becoming enlightened
just to kill the sudden pain

and falling into bliss
of blindness again.

Luang Prabang

There is no acupuncture point
for a single mosquito bite.

ARUSHA

A group of drums
is gathered in the radiance
of the baobab tree.

The sun is slowly bleeding out

in all its gore and majesty.
I still love the darkness

as much when as a child
I feared to be extracted
out of its opposition.

KANYAKUMARI

In the junction of three names
for a single ocean,
you found our room
more dingy
than me.
Embodiment of life,

this is my flesh —
thirst and I will drown.

Robben Island

The ocean is cold
because so many penguins
swim in it.

Hammer rocks of propaganda

with the pulse of your heart
to scatter a flint of truth
out of it.

Calcutta

Take care
and give it
away.

There is a different set of rules
for the pawns
and the kings.

For the pawns here is not even a chance
to be resurrected, for the kings
to be killed.

Take-away
and give care
to it.

LIVINGSTONE

My mother is death
and I have three sisters and three brothers,
I am number three.

My father is also in the grave.
I have one child, a boy
who is living with my aunt.

I love singing and dancing,
and my favorite band is called Westlife.

I have a boyfriend,
but I will not marry him
or anybody else either,
because some men don't
appreciate woman. I am a women.

Give me 20.000 kwacha, I need
to buy some nshima for breakfast.

MOMBASA

Hello, how are you?
I am fine, and you?

Me am also fine. Are you married?
Not right now, I am divorced.
Do you have a girlfriend then?
Yes I do.
Do you have girlfriend in Africa then?
No I don't.
Maybe me can be your girlfriend in Kenya then, yes?
Thank you for your offer, but no thank you.

Would you like to be my family friend then?
What does it mean?
It's a friend who gives money to me
and my husband, but there is no sex.
Ah... okay, thank you,
but I am not interested,
sorry for that.

No, it's okay, have a nice day.
You too.

Mumbai

Travelling is a strong way
to learn how to let go.

You are just one
set of worn-out lungs
for second-hand oxygen,
in this kaleidoscope
of multiple senses,

rattling like a mechanical door
waiting for its final stop.

Mamallapuram

Squeezing through the roof
of the root of the world
where a turquoise breeze
still reigns.

'Launch your parachute
of life our beloved child',
my grandparents, still unearthed
repeatedly chant.

MYSORE

My world in your mind,
your body in my world;

the outskirts of opposites
of same thought.

LALIBELA

I remember these clouds, evolving

mountains over there.
I had to be at home.

II

ERTA ALE

When a mountain peak
desires to be on the same level
with the others,

it erupts.

Lying low then
for a few millennia
at the five million star Hilton.

JAISALMER

Stars above
and underneath.
Camels are resting
on the pixels of the desert –
full display of grace.

Monkey Bay

The weather is pleasant and plausible quiet.
Only at the table of Vikings
normal blah-blah is going on, where to
head tomorrow.
I am not in such a rush,

just thinking on my own.
What are you 'sinking about',
this German repeats?
Just how ice cap melts slowly
in the glass of gin and tonic.

Hampi

Friends we made, good
friends we were, loved ones
we left behind.
In the boulderscape of the self
our memory roams between slabs of ice-
cream and sun.

BANGKOK

In the coffee shop
waitress winked at me.
What is that supposed to mean
– memento mori?

When Brahman winks
I wink no more

and you can ship my bones
to the country
code which I keep repeating
over and over again.

Addis Abeba

Her English vocabulatory was limited
to one irrefutable word 'enjoy',
and mine Amharic wasn't much broader either.
So we did what was to be done – enjoyed ourselves

accordingly the universal language
of dance, drinks and laugh
as archangels of evolution

towards nothing –
new flowers of the present.

HOGSBACK

Every poem is a translation
before it is composed.

Then it clarifies itself
like a mist
out of the hog's back

Soweto

Rhythm is ultimate product.

Except that you can blame
white heterosexual male

for everything.
Below him is the only god

to whom you keep dancing for.

MAPUTO

Rasta don't live in the streets,

Rasta lives in the corners.
Rasta don't hate a police,
Rasta go with the flow.

Rasta don't work,
Rasta organize.
Rasta don't have money,

Rasta use it all.
Rasta don't die,
Rasta relax.

I and I, Rastafari.

Johannesburg

I didn't seek freedom,
it was just a working title

for indigenous peace process.

There is no other god
and myth was his only son.

Dar Es Salaam

When one kindled a candle
on the operation table of reason,
we appeared immediately at the twilight
of the perennial question: who are you
the veiled one

and who is asking?

Black hole sun, Aurora
consurgens, do you have an
apt expression for such controversy?
This artery I am holding
against your knife

for peace.

Santa Paloma

In Garden of Eden
there is no separation
for horses nor zebras.
In Republic of Imagination
there is no other declaration
for the world but the word itself.

And in there we will embed
our first city.

CAPE TOWN

In the middle of the name
is acceptance, cradle of good hope
for a human-

kind like me.
What really triggers the process of chance?
Is it love or the death

of it,
I don't know. But
I still hold a fear

that it will be just another persona
like the rest of us
are for you.

Varkala

Without a dot no circle
can be drawn, triangle formed
or square constructed.
Without a center point
one cannot stage forms harmoniously.

The trick is to make the point invisible
to the forms emanating
from it
for her own delight.

Parga

Great white bullet hole
on a pitch black wall,
space between your lips

in the private eye's dream.

Wedding coffin
for a groom
is about to be sold.

CHITRAKOOT

Soul of the man is the body of the god.
Soul of the god is the mind of the dog,
the strive of the seed in the soil.

Who knows
about the spirit of the dog,
will it ascend to the heaven
or will it continue to chase the tales of the god
on the ground?
I assume that

every now and then
enlightened one needs to become darkened
to obtain mehr licht
to his gaze.

CAPE AGULHAS

Forgiveness is the most difficult form
of lying, being almost opposite
of it. Highest degree of love
is just to love

no more.
These lines of seaweed

are held hostage
by you,
until the next tide.
Farther.

Kampala

I am ready to fall in love
away from here
where a man carries his pen
as a token of prestige
and not as a dagger.

Poem is a thriller
where the reader murders
its author.

Mäyry

We avoid risks in life
to make it safe
for the death to catch up.

Summer is gone.
It's time to saddle up!

Life is a proposal
not a statement
to put your name under.

Table of contents

I

II